Story of My
F*cking Life

A Journal for
Banishing the Bullsh*t,
Unlocking Your Creativity,
and Celebrating the
Absurdity of Life

JASON MUSTIAN

CASTLE POINT BOOKS
NEW YORK

www.castlepointbooks.com

The Castle Point Books trademark is owned by Castle Point Publishing, LLC.
Castle Point books are published and distributed by St. Martin's Publishing Group.

ISBN 978-1-250-27548-6 (trade paperback)

Illustrations by Jason Mustian

Our books may be purchased in bulk for promotional, educational, or business use.
Please contact your local bookseller or the Macmillan Corporate and
Premium Sales Department at 1-800-221-7945, extension 5442, or by email at
MacmillanSpecialMarkets@macmillan.com.

First Edition: 2021

10 9 8 7 6 5 4 3 2 1

THIS FUCKING LIFE BELONGS TO:

_____

INTRODUCTION

I HOPE THIS JOURNAL FINDS YOU WELL. ‹WINK.› But especially
if it doesn't, you're in the right place to find a little fucking
inner peace.

Story of My F*cking Life, based on my Instagram account
@StoryOfMyFuckingLife, gives you a place to sound off about
how life can be a real shitshow sometimes—without getting
arrested or left with zero followers on social. No matter where
the absurdity abounds in your life—from relationships and
adulting to finances and work, you'll find the creative pages
ahead are a profanity-laden release and bright spot of sanity in
your day. Enjoy the universal truths in my book cover art, then
let journaling prompts guide you to tell your own damn truth.

WHAT'S THE BIGGEST LINE OF BULLSHIT
you've heard in the past few days?

WHAT WORDS FELT REAL AS HELL TO YOU LATELY?

Too Late For Coffee, Too Early For Vodka:

How To Make It Through The Afternoon

WHAT SURVIVAL GUIDE ARE YOU LIVING RIGHT NOW,
and what brings you at least a few moments of
fucking sanity as you push through?

WHAT QUESTIONS (BIG AND LITTLE) ARE HAUNTING YOU RIGHT NOW? Let that shit go— release all your inner ramblings right here.

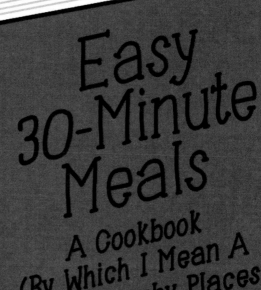

Easy 30-Minute Meals

A Cookbook
(By Which I Mean A List Of Nearby Places That Offer DoorDash)

WHAT EXPECTATIONS SET BY OTHERS OR YOURSELF ARE DRIVING YOU INSANE?

How can you reasonably lower them?

HERE'S YOUR SPACE TO GET BRUTALLY HONEST.
What have you great'ed that there's no chance in hell you'll carry through with?
(Attach more paper as needed.)

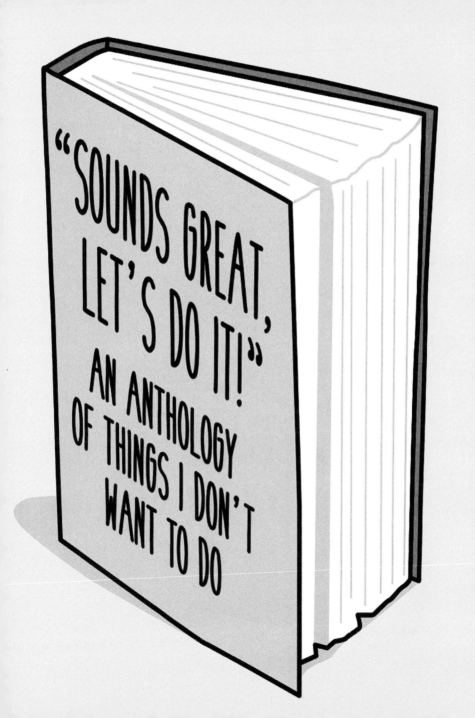

THE YOGA BALL

Not Only Will I Never Use It, I Can't Even Pile Laundry On It

WHAT'S NO LONGER SERVING YOU BUT TAKING UP PRECIOUS SPACE? How can you let it gently roll out of your life or give it a swift kick?

WHAT DO YOU FEAR OTHER PEOPLE THINK OR SAY ABOUT YOU, and how is it holding you back from bright, shining possibilities?

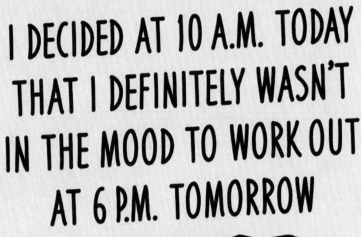

I DECIDED AT 10 A.M. TODAY
THAT I DEFINITELY WASN'T
IN THE MOOD TO WORK OUT
AT 6 P.M. TOMORROW

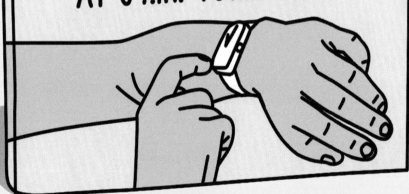

SOME DECISIONS ARE SIMPLE AS FUCK;
others take a little more thought.
What decision is long overdue in your life?
Make it now, no take-backs.

WHO DO YOU GO TO WHEN YOU WANT TO HEAR THAT YOU'RE ABSOLUTELY FUCKING RIGHT
and need a vote of confidence?

WHO CAN YOU GO TO WHEN YOU NEED TO HEAR THAT YOU'RE ABSOLUTELY FUCKING WRONG
(because you kind of already know deep down)?

HOW TO WIN FRIENDS

(Who Tell You What You Want To Hear)

& INFLUENCE PEOPLE

(Who Already Agree With You On Everything)

A Guide To Modern Discourse

There Should
Be No Room For
Hate In Our Hearts
Except For When It
Comes To People
Who Stand Up On
Airplanes As Soon
As They Land

WHAT LITTLE THINGS (IN THE GREATER SCHEME) DO OTHER PEOPLE DO THAT PISS YOU OFF?

List your top 20 here. Then share a copy with friends, so they know better.

NO MATTER HOW FUCKING RIDICULOUS IT MAY SOUND TO SOMEONE ELSE, what's one reasonable goal you can accomplish today?

DAMMIT, I FORGOT TO DO THE THING I UNLOCKED MY PHONE TO DO (AGAIN)
SEQUEL TO THE HIT NOVEL FROM 5 MINUTES AGO: DAMMIT, I FORGOT TO DO THE THING I UNLOCKED MY PHONE TO DO

CHOOSE YOUR OWN ADVENTURE
I CAN EITHER DISAPPOINT YOU TRADITIONALLY OR WE CAN DEVELOP A CUSTOMIZED PLAN THAT FITS YOUR NEEDS

WHO ARE YOU TERRIFIED OF DISAPPOINTING?

Who have you already disappointed enough that you have adequately lowered their expectations?

WHAT SPECIAL, BUT STUPID, SKILLS
get you far in life?

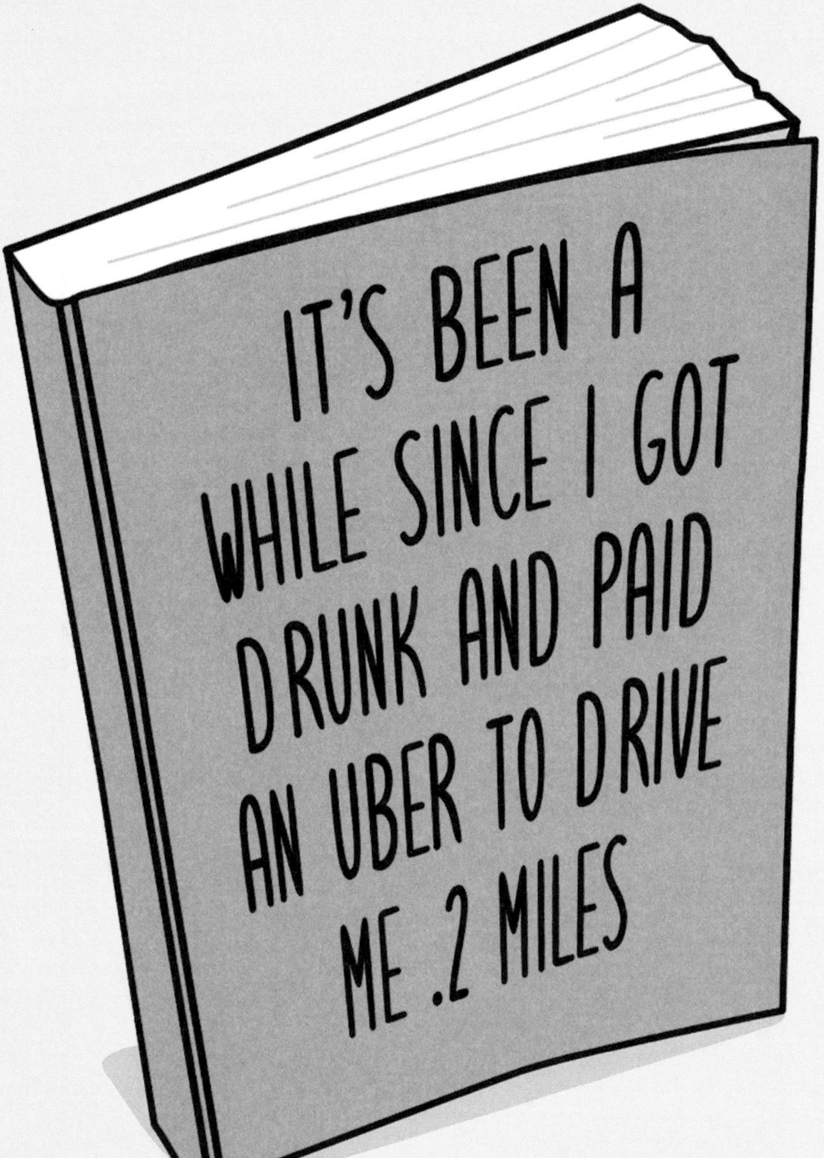
IT'S BEEN A
WHILE SINCE I GOT
DRUNK AND PAID
AN UBER TO DRIVE
ME .2 MILES

WHAT THINGS HAVE YOU DONE IN THE PAST YEAR THAT SEEM CRAZY ON PAPER but gave you great satisfaction? Circle or highlight the ones worth doing again soon.

SOMETIMES SHITTY SITUATIONS BRING PERMISSION FOR NO PANTS AND SHOWER WINE.

What rays of sunshine have you discovered under totally unexpected circumstances?

I'm Looking Forward
To Everything Getting
Back To Normal,
But I'm Gonna Miss
Morning Shower Wine

Book IV of
The Quarantine
Chronicles Saga

TRUE BEAUTY COMES FROM WITHIN

AND OTHER MANTRAS FOR WHEN YOU SEE YOURSELF IN THE VIDEO WINDOW OF A ZOOM CALL

WHAT INSECURITIES DO YOU NEED TO SQUASH OR AT LEAST OWN UP TO? What could your don't-give-a-damn mantra be?

WHAT WORRIES ARE FLOODING YOUR MIND RIGHT NOW?
Let the dam open below, then cross out the ones
that aren't worth an ounce of your fucking energy.

"No Worries"

A COMPENDIUM OF THINGS THAT ARE ACTUALLY VERY MUCH WORRIES

CHOOSE YOUR
OWN ADVENTURE

DEALING WITH MY GLARING EMOTIONAL ISSUES OR CONTINUING TO FILL MY APARTMENT WITH SUCCULENTS

WHEN YOU'RE LOOKING TO ESCAPE FOR A FEW MINUTES—OR HOURS—WHAT DO YOU BURY YOURSELF IN? Does it work?

WHAT TASK SEEMS NEVER-ENDING IN YOUR LIFE?
Is it worth pushing through to get it done or is there room to settle at good-e-fucking-nough?

I Never Feel More
Accomplished Than When
I Do A Load Of Laundry
And I Never Feel Less
Accomplished Than When
I Leave That Load Of
Laundry In A Pile On
My Floor For 6 Weeks

A MEMOIR

WHAT SITUATION OR PERSON IS GUARANTEED
to exhaust you every time?

WHAT ENERGIZES YOU AND BRINGS YOU BACK
to a great (or at least, manageable) mood again?

LIFE IS FULL OF MYSTERIES.
What are the latest you have faced that feel a little like bullshit?

TALES FROM A
TIME/SPACE PARADOX
I SENT MY FRIEND A
4-MINUTE YOUTUBE VIDEO
AND THEY REPLIED "NICE" 17
SECONDS AFTER I SENT IT

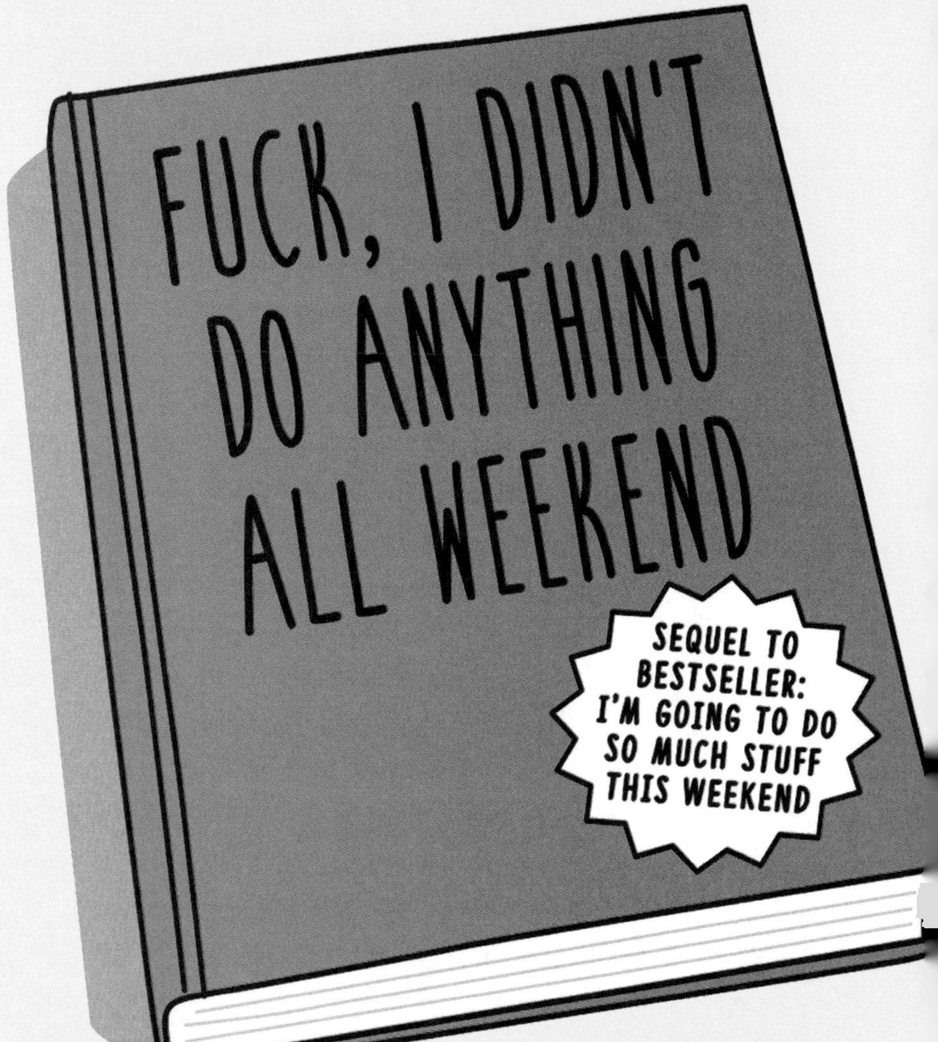
FUCK, I DIDN'T DO ANYTHING ALL WEEKEND
SEQUEL TO BESTSELLER: I'M GOING TO DO SO MUCH STUFF THIS WEEKEND

WHAT HASN'T TURNED OUT AS PLANNED THIS WEEK
but was actually just what you needed?

IN WHAT PARTS OF YOUR LIFE ARE YOU EXHAUSTED FROM FAKING IT AND READY TO COME CLEAN—
no matter what others say or think?

Kjlkmbb, backspace backspace backspace backspace, fnnnnff backspace backspace And Other Texts I've Faked Writing To Avoid Having To Have A Social Interaction

"SEE, LIKE I SAID,
IT'S IN THE DRAWER"

Incredibly Gratifying Sequel
To The Marital Thriller
"I Checked The Drawer, It's Not There"

WHAT WORDS DO YOU FEEL LIKE YOU SAY ON REPEAT BECAUSE NO ONE FUCKING LISTENS?

Is it time to raise the volume or is it more fun to watch them amble around like idiots?

IN WHAT AREAS OF YOUR LIFE DO YOU HAVE EVERYONE FOOLED, thinking you have your shit together?

....
....
....
....
....
....
....
....

WHAT ARE THE TELLS OTHERS AREN'T AS PUT-TOGETHER AS YOU MIGHT SUSPECT?

....
....
....
....
....
....
....
....
....
....

ALL MY LAUNDRY
— IS FOLDED —

And Other Signs That
Seemingly Indicate I've
Got My Life Together
But Are Really Signs I'm
Procrastinating Having
A Nervous Breakdown

CHOOSE YOUR
OWN ADVENTURE

THINGS ARE GOING REALLY GREAT RIGHT NOW, HOW DO YOU WANT TO FUCK IT UP?

WHAT'S THE BIGGEST DISASTER YOU'VE EXPERIENCED LATELY? Did any of the pieces survive or did you start building back from scratch?

WOULD YOU MAKE A DIFFERENT MOVE IF YOU HAD TO DO IT ALL OVER AGAIN?

WHAT *NEVER, EVER* HAPPENED IN YOUR LIFE?
No witnesses, no proof, and you've moved past
the statute of limitations in your mind.

My Google Search History Is 85% Me Poorly Spelling Simple Words So I Can Copy And Paste The Proper Spelling Into An Email

FOR BETTER OR FOR WORSE, WHAT WOULD YOUR GOOGLE SEARCH HISTORY REVEAL ABOUT YOU?

IS THERE ANYONE YOU WOULD GIVE PERMISSION TO VIEW IT? Who would you guard it from at all costs?

WHAT'S THE MOST INSANE MEETING (BUSINESS OR PERSONAL) YOU'VE BEEN A PART OF?
Were you alone in your desire to flee?

Principles Of Business Management

How To Call A Meeting To Find Out When Everyone Is Available For The Next Meeting

Encyclopedia

OF MOVIES & TV SHOWS
PEOPLE TOLD ME I SHOULD
ADD TO MY WATCH LIST
AND I TOLD THEM I
WOULD ADD TO MY WATCH
LIST BUT I'M NOT GOING
TO ADD THEM TO MY
WATCH LIST

Ba-Bb

WHAT GUILTY PLEASURES ARE UNIQUELY YOU AND MAKE YOU PROUD TO DECLARE,

"Yes, I'm *still* watching!"?

WHAT PHYSICAL ACCOMPLISHMENTS (OR LACK OF) WOULD QUALIFY YOU AS A RECORD HOLDER
or at least get you a stellar participation trophy?

Holding My Breath
While Walking Uphill
So Strangers Don't
Hear Me Fighting
For My Life
———————
A FITNESS MEMOIR

I Just Gotta
Get Past This
Last Hard Week
And Then It's
Smooth Sailing

BOOK 1 OF 1,584,498

WHAT EXPERT LIES DO YOU TELL YOURSELF
AND HONESTLY BELIEVE EVERY TIME—
for the good of your mental health?

WHAT'S THE CRAZIEST THING YOU'VE EVER SPENT WAY TOO MUCH FUCKING MONEY ON?
Would you do it again?

SHITTY FINANCIAL MANAGEMENT FOR BEGINNERS

I JUST SPENT $25 ON AN $8.79 MEAL FROM UBER EATS

GRAB YOUR PHONE. WHAT CAREFULLY STAGED PHOTOS BRING YOU SO MUCH FUCKING JOY AND PRIDE?

WHAT PHOTOS TAKEN ACCIDENTALLY OR UNEXPECTEDLY BRING YOU SHAME? How can you get over yourself enough to find joy in them anyway?

WHAT GREAT ACTS OF PROCRASTINATION
or avoidance are destined to pop up in your memoir?

I'M IN SURPRISINGLY GOOD SHAPE FOR SOMEONE WHO CANCELS AT LEAST 5 ONLINE ORDERS PER WEEK BECAUSE MY CREDIT CARD IS IN ANOTHER ROOM

ORDER CANCEL

A MEMOIR

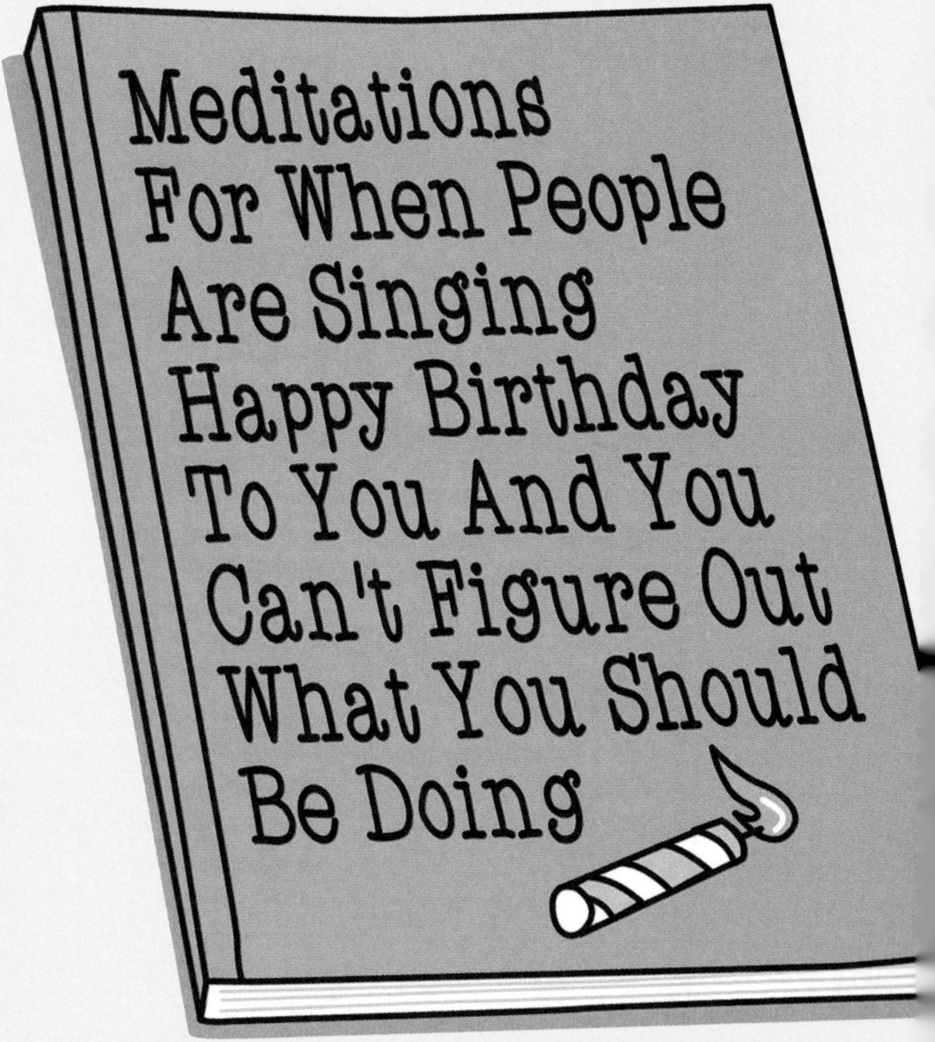
Meditations
For When People
Are Singing
Happy Birthday
To You And You
Can't Figure Out
What You Should
Be Doing

WHAT DILEMMAS (BIG AND LITTLE) ARE YOU TRYING TO FIGURE OUT THIS WEEK? Consider your options—which might include just sitting still and smiling through the pain.

WHAT OR WHO WOULD YOU DRIVE MILES OUT OF YOUR WAY—through hell or high water—**TO AVOID?**

WHAT OR WHO WOULD YOU DRIVE MILES OUT OF YOUR WAY—through hell or high water—**TO SEE?**

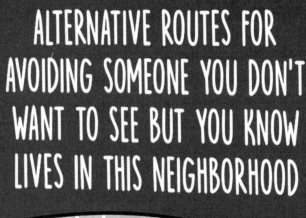
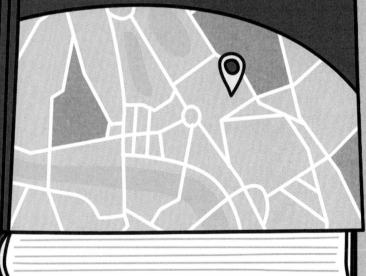

KGo_pufAdf1031u0316.jpg
And Other Files
I Want To Keep But
Apparently Never
Want To Find Again

WHAT ARE YOU TRYING TO REDISCOVER IN YOUR LIFE?

WHAT ARE YOU COMPLETELY OK WITH NEVER RELIVING AGAIN?

WHAT MOMENT OF UTTER STRESS OR FEAR TURNED OUT FUCKING FINE IN THE END?

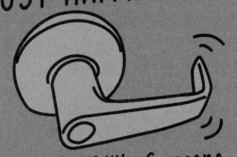

WHAT SITUATION HAVE YOU USED
SMOOTH MOVES TO GET OUT OF LATELY?

GO AHEAD AND CATASTROPHIZE ANY DAY OF THE WEEK—NOT JUST SUNDAY. What are the worst things that could happen this week?

NOW, CROSS OUT ANYTHING THAT SEEMS SLIM AND SHADY in the light of reality.

HYPOTHETICAL UNPLEASANT SITUATIONS THAT COULD POSSIBLY HAPPEN THIS WEEK

—

A SUNDAY EVENING MEDITATION

2019
2020
2021

Is Going To Be The Year
I Get My Life Together

A MEMOIR

WHAT DOES GETTING YOUR LIFE TOGETHER LOOK LIKE FOR YOU? Is it more memoir or fantasy?

WHAT "NICE" THING HAVE YOU DONE LATELY THAT MIGHT HAVE ALSO BENEFITED YOU?

Confess it all–there's no shame in self-care!

THE ONLY REASON I BROUGHT THIS NICE OF A BOTTLE OF WINE TO YOUR PARTY WAS BECAUSE I WAS PLANNING ON DRINKING IT
A MEMOIR

SAID "LOOKS GREAT, THANK YOU SO MUCH!" AND STILL TIPPED GENEROUSLY AFTER GETTING A TERRIBLE HAIRCUT
A COLLECTION OF TIMES I DIDN'T STAND UP FOR MYSELF
VOL 1 of 500

WHEN DO YOU REGRET NOT STANDING UP FOR YOURSELF?

....

....

....

....

....

....

....

WHEN DID YOU EARN A FUCKING GOLD MEDAL FOR HOW FAR UP YOU STOOD?
Hear the inner applause as you write.

....

....

....

....

....

....

....

....

WHEN WAS THE LAST TIME YOU THREW CAUTION TO THE WIND and your standards out the window so you could fucking enjoy yourself?

GREAT WORKS
of SELF-DELUSION

I Know I Shouldn't Cut
My Own Bangs Again,
But This Time It'll
Turn Out Well

WHAT HAVE YOU DONE LATELY AGAINST YOUR OWN BETTER JUDGMENT? Who do you need to call next time before you make this tragic leap?

THINK OF A TIME WHEN YOU MADE LEMONADE OUT OF LEMONS and went on your fucking way.

Having Scrambled Eggs Again Because I Fucked Up Making An Omelet
A Cookbook

WHAT DO YOU LOSE ALL TRACK OF TIME DOING?
Make a plan to get lost in something mindless and enjoyable this week.

WHAT PERCENTAGE OF YOUR WORKDAY
do you spend on extraneous bullshit?

WHAT MAKES IT ALL WORTHWHILE?

"WE'VE UPDATED
OUR PRIVACY POLICY"
Vol 1 of 1,000,000
in the GDPR Emails Series

WHY DID I DO THAT?

A NOVEL BY ME

With Guest Appearances
By A Fifth Glass Of Wine
When I Was Already Pretty
Drunk At Two

WHEN HAVE YOUR ACTIONS LEFT YOU
WITH A HANGOVER OF REGRET?

....

....

....

....

....

....

....

....

WHO DOESN'T GIVE A SHIT WHAT YOU DO
AND LOVES YOU ANYWAY?

....

....

....

....

....

....

....

....

WHAT WAS THE LAST CONVERSATION YOU HAD WITH YOURSELF? What came out of it?

HYPOTHETICAL ARGUMENTS I'VE WON IN THE SHOWER

VOL 1 OF 16

PROFILES IN COURAGE:
Actually Showing Up To Plans
I Made A Week Ago
KNOCK
KNOCK

WHAT'S THE MOST EMOTIONALLY BADASS THING YOU'VE EVER DONE?

WHAT'S THE MOST PHYSICALLY BADASS THING YOU'VE EVER DONE?

THERE'S A CONSPIRACY THEORY FOR EVERYBODY.

What has you *this* close to mapping
a mess of string on your wall?

GREAT MYSTERIES OF OUR TIME:
I said something out loud 3 days ago and now I'm seeing ads for it on Facebook

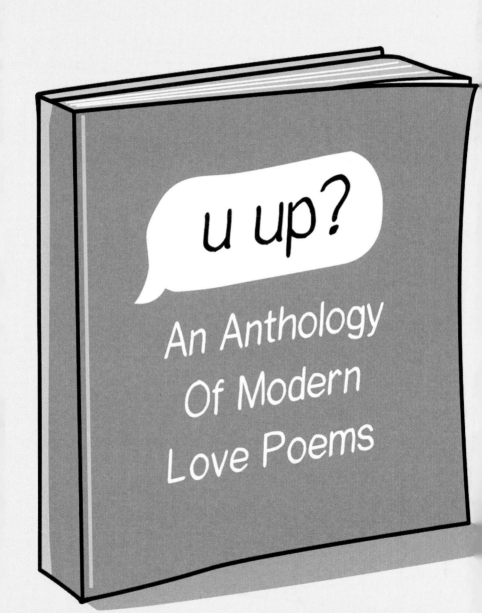

WHAT'S THE LEAST ROMANTIC THING
YOU'VE EVER PRETENDED TO LIKE?

WHEN HAVE YOU OPTED FOR HONESTY OVER BULLSHIT?

WHEN HAVE YOU SURPRISED YOURSELF WITH YOUR OWN HANDIWORK?

....

....

....

....

....

....

....

....

WHEN HAVE YOU SURPRISED YOURSELF WITH YOUR INEPTITUDE?

....

....

....

....

....

....

....

....

....

SIMPLE HOME IMPROVEMENT PROJECTS
YOU CAN START YOURSELF BUT INEVITABLY CALL A PROFESSIONAL TO FINISH ONCE YOU FUCK IT UP

SHARE A SOCIAL-MEDIA NIGHTMARE
that happened to you and how you escaped.

IF YOU COULD ONLY LISTEN TO SIX SONGS FOR THE REST OF YOUR LIFE, WHAT WOULD THEY BE?

What's the significance behind each?

WHY DO I EVEN PAY FOR A PREMIUM SPOTIFY ACCOUNT WHEN I JUST LISTEN TO THE SAME 6 SONGS EVERY DAY?

AND OTHER REFLECTIONS

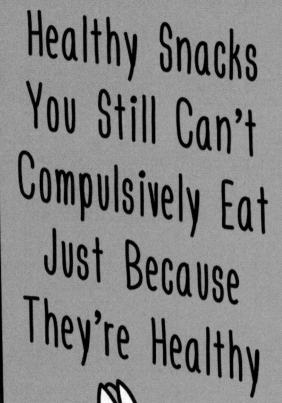

Healthy Snacks You Still Can't Compulsively Eat Just Because They're Healthy

WHAT GOOD HABITS DO YOU HAVE TO
TALK YOURSELF INTO DOING?
When has that worked and not worked?

HOW WOULD YOU CHARACTERIZE
YOUR RELATIONSHIP TO YOUR JOB?
Would you say you work too much or too little?

The 4-Hour Workweek

(IN THE SENSE THAT I'M
ONLY DOING 4 HOURS OF ACTUAL
WORK THIS WEEK, BECAUSE THEY
HONESTLY DON'T PAY
ME ENOUGH TO DO MORE)

HOW TO ADMIT YOU'RE WRONG WHILE STILL IMPLYING THEY'RE WRONGER

WHO IS WAITING FOR YOUR CONFESSION THAT YOU WERE (GULP) WRONG?

WHO STILL OWES YOU AN APOLOGY?

WHAT UNUSUAL THINGS IN YOUR LIFE BRING YOU AN ODD SENSE OF SATISFACTION?

Better Than Sex

A MEMOIR OF EACH TIME
I TELL MY SPOUSE WHERE
SOMETHING IS AND THEY
SAY IT'S NOT THERE BUT
I GO AND FIND IT EXACTLY
WHERE I SAID IT WAS
AND HAND IT TO THEM

WHAT UNFINISHED BUSINESS NEEDS YOUR ATTENTION?

WHAT UNFINISHED BUSINESS DO YOU NEED TO LET GO?

WHAT URGENT ANSWERS—from Google or another source—DO YOU NEED TO HEAR RIGHT NOW?

CHOOSE YOUR
OWN ADVENTURE

GOOGLING WHETHER THERE'S SOMETHING WRONG WITH YOU OR NOT WRONG WITH YOU, DEPENDING ON WHAT YOU NEED TO HEAR RIGHT NOW

IF YOU COULD ESCAPE FROM YOUR LIFE FOR A DAY,
what story line from a book, show,
or movie would you want to live?

IS THERE ANY PART OF THIS FICTION
YOU CAN BRING TO YOUR REAL LIFE?

WHAT CHANGES SEND YOU INTO A COMPLETE SPIRAL?

....

....

....

....

....

....

....

....

....

WHAT CHANGES SPARK YOUR CREATIVITY?

....

....

....

....

....

....

....

....

....

....

Introduction to Clowning

Buying $17 Salads

WHAT'S THE MOST OVER-THE-TOP THING YOU'VE DONE TO JUMP ON A TREND?

When was your moment of realization?

WHAT ARE THE CRAZY CIRCLES OF DRAMA OR ANXIETY IN YOUR LIFE? Is there a way to jump off the fucking merry-go-round?

Lying To My Therapist
Makes My Therapy
Pointless, But The Fact
That I Lie To My Therapist
Underscores How Much
I Really Need Therapy

A Paradox

MEDITATIONS FOR
WHEN YOU'RE NOT RICH
ENOUGH TO LIVE LIFE
WITHOUT WORRY

WHAT WORRIES WOULD YOU DROP-KICK
into oblivion if you could?

WHEN HAVE YOU SPENT WAY TOO MUCH TIME OR EFFORT TRYING TO GET SOMEONE'S APPROVAL?
How can you come to your fucking senses and stop doing that?

HOW TO SPEND $50K ON 100 INSTAGRAM LIKES

A Guide To Planning A Wedding

WALKING THE LINE BETWEEN SELF-DESTRUCTION AND SELF-CARE

A MEMOIR

WHAT DO YOU NEED TO TAKE A PAUSE FROM THIS WEEK so you can regain your balance and avoid tumbling into a void of despair?

WHEN WAS THE LAST TIME "NO PROBLEM" BECAME A PROBLEM? If you could go back in time, what would your response be?

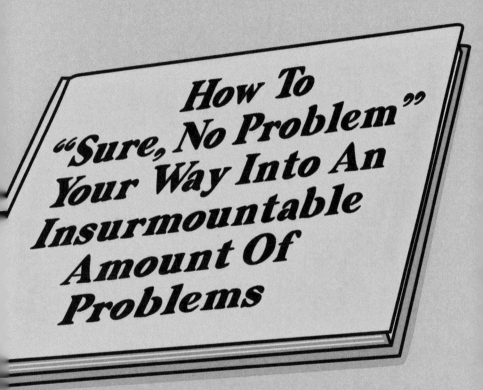

How To
"Sure, No Problem"
Your Way Into An
Insurmountable
Amount Of
Problems

1,001

THINGS I DON'T ACTUALLY WANT YOUR INPUT ON

A Guide To Asking Your Partner For Their Input

WHAT DO YOU THINK YOU SHOULD BE FREE TO RANT ABOUT AS MUCH AS YOU WANT? Give an example of unsolicited advice from your recent past.

FROM PRACTICAL ("What's that fucking password?") TO POETIC (how the sky looked *that* day), WHAT ARE 10 THINGS YOU WANT TO REMEMBER?

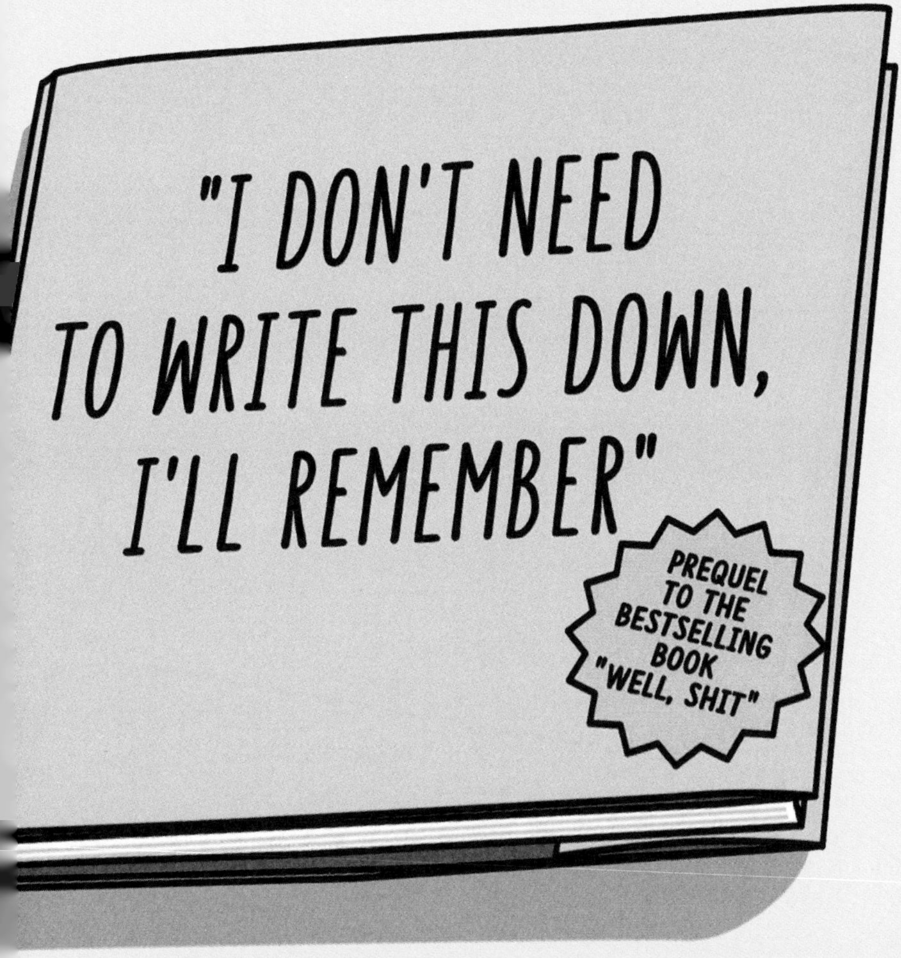
"I DON'T NEED TO WRITE THIS DOWN, I'LL REMEMBER"
PREQUEL TO THE BESTSELLING BOOK "WELL, SHIT"

YOUR BOOK TITLE HERE

YOUR STORY HERE...

YOUR BOOK
TITLE HERE

YOUR STORY HERE...

YOUR BOOK TITLE HERE

YOUR STORY HERE...

YOUR
BOOK
TITLE
HERE

YOUR STORY HERE...

ACKNOWLEDGMENTS

MY MOST SINCERE GRATITUDE to Cole Mitchell, without whom I would never have created the @storyofmyfuckinglife account. Thank you to anyone who has submitted a book cover, including but not limited to Jake Currie, Mike Primavera, Hannah Riley, Dan Wilbur, and Nate Armbruster. Big ups to Jennifer Leight, Katie Jennings, and St. Martin's Press for convincing me to get off my ass and do this book. And last but not least, to those who follow @storyofmyfuckinglife, I will never forget you, unless you unfollow, and then you are dead to me.

The Big Book of People Who Helped Make This Book Possible And Will Be Blamed Entirely If It Is Not A Total Success

STAY IN TOUCH

Keep looking on the humorous side of life with @StoryOfMyFuckingLife! Feeling inspired? Submit your best book cover lines using the hashtag #storyofmyfuckinglife.